Original title:
The Art of Ice Skating...Badly

Copyright © 2024 Creative Arts Management OÜ
All rights reserved.

Author: Ronan Whitfield
ISBN HARDBACK: 978-9916-94-272-7
ISBN PAPERBACK: 978-9916-94-273-4

Whirling Dervishes of the Rink

Spinning like tops on a shiny floor,
Feet tangled up, oh, we laugh and roar.
Arms flailing wildly, a wobbly show,
Who knew that gliding could be this slow?

Twists and turns with a goofy grace,
A delightful dance, a frosty chase.
A penguin parade, we slide and fall,
Each tumble becomes a viral call!

Frozen Fun and Flawed Flair

Slip and slide like it's a game,
Every wobble feels the same.
Balance is just a myth up here,
We giggle loud, dispel the fear.

One foot forward, two feet back,
Break the silence with a whack!
Flailing limbs in bright attire,
Making memories we admire!

The Ballet of Awkward Awesomeness

A pirouette that goes all wrong,
We laugh together, sing our song.
With stiffened knees and silly grace,
We twirl and stumble in this space.

A grand jete, or is it a fall?
Each leap, a laugh, we have a ball.
Choreographed by chance and glee,
Our rhythmic chaos sets us free!

Comically Cruising on Icebound Paths

Gliding forth with clumsy charm,
A friendly shout, alarmed no harm.
Beneath the lights, we sway and gleam,
A slippery path becomes our dream.

Wobbly figures, skating free,
Who knew the show was to be me?
From one edge to the other we roam,
Laughing aloud, we feel at home!

Blunders in a Beautiful Freeze

Twirl and spin, oh what a sight,
My feet have taken quite the flight.
A graceful leap? Nope, not today,
I'm just a snowman in disarray.

Wobbling like I'm on a boat,
Each glide feels like a heavy coat.
I crash and slide, oh what a thrill,
But laughter chases any chill.

Slips and Slides of a Shaky Heart

I took a step, my knees went weak,
Like a chicken, I began to squeak.
With each uncertain leap and fall,
I shall conquer—no, not at all!

The sound of laughter shakes the air,
As I skate like I haven't a care.
Oh, what a mess, yet I feel fine,
With every faceplant, I still shine.

Tiptoeing Through the Icebound Slipstream

Tiptoe here, tiptoe there,
Spin around—oh, do take care!
Like a deer upon the ice,
Trying hard, I pay the price.

Swaying left, then to the right,
Decisions made in sheer delight.
A well-timed push, a dizzying whir,
As I flail like a blender with a purr.

Laughter Echoes on the Rink

Round and round, the circle flows,
A chilli crop of graceful woes.
I twirl, I spin, my world's a blur,
This icy trip? Such a wild stir!

With every crash, I earn a cheer,
Every stumble brings good cheer.
As laughter rings and spirits soar,
I bravely slide, then down I floor.

Choreography of Clumsy Twirls

With a hop and a skip, I hit the rink,
My legs like spaghetti, I can hardly think.
Spinning around, what a sight to see,
Gravity's my foe, yet I'm wild and free.

My arms flail about, just like a bird,
Each graceful attempt, completely absurd.
Twisting and turning, I'm all out of sync,
But giggles and laughter take over the stink.

Frozen Dreams and Epic Falls

I dream of the glide, so smooth and so fine,
But alas, I look more like a tangled line.
With each epic fall, I hear laughter bloom,
As I land on my back with a loud, "Kaboom!"

The skates are my friends, or so I once thought,
Until they conspired to make me distraught.
With a twist and a trip, I'm down on the ice,
Life's full of adventure, oh, ain't it nice?

Wobbly Elegance on Thin Ice

Elegance wobbles on my icy path,
Each move a gamble, I feel the wrath.
Like a graceful swan, or perhaps a goat,
My elegance falters; I silently gloat.

I teeter, I totter, my balance at stake,
A figure skater? More like a quaking quake.
With a plunge and a splash, I embrace the cold,
In this circus of ice, I'm brave and bold.

Dance of the Unbalanced Blades

Unbalanced blades make a loud, clumsy sound,
As my body performs a chaotic round.
With a whirl and a twirl, I attempt to be grand,
But instead, I wind up face-first in the sand.

The ice becomes my stage, a slippery floor,
As I leap like a fish, a strange kind of lore.
With a chuckle and cheer, the crowd can't resist,
In this world of chaos, I simply persist.

Potholes in a Winter Wonderland

Skates on my feet, oh what a sight,
I glide like a duck, but not quite right.
Wobbling here, and spinning there,
I charm the crowd with my frosty flair.

I hit a bump, I start to fly,
My flailing arms whisper goodbye.
With each tumble, laughter fills the air,
Snowflakes applaud my comic flair.

Spirals of Awkward Splendor

Twisting and turning like a clumsy baller,
I pirouette once, then give a holler.
Two left feet, but heart full of glee,
The ice is my stage; I'm wild and free.

A graceful arc? Not in my grasp,
I spin and I flop, what a fun rasp.
Watch as I dive, it's quite the show,
An accidental master of the fall and flow.

A Frigid Ballet of Missteps

The spotlight shines on my awkward form,
With every skid, I bring the charm.
A leap and a lurch, then down I go,
My ice-bound ballet is quite the show.

Each misstep's met with infectious cheer,
As friends around me all draw near.
My routines are wild, my landings fraught,
Yet laughter erupts with each slip and thought.

Ice Rink Antics and Wipeouts

Here I am, cloaked in winter's glow,
But graceful? That's not my tempo.
With each awkward stride, I take my chance,
To turn every wobble into a dance.

Down I go, with a dramatic flair,
Flopping like snowman with a busted chair.
The crowd erupts in roars of delight,
I bow with a grin, what a goofy sight!

Embracing the Icy Embrace of Fumbles

With blades that slide and twist around,
I spin and fall without a sound.
My graceful moves, a sight to see,
But mostly I just crash with glee.

A pirouette that turns to fling,
My limbs will flop; oh what a thing!
The rink's a stage, my epic fail,
Like fish on land, I flail and wail.

Frigid Fantasy of the Awkward

In a world of glimmer and frost,
I glide along, but I'm the cost.
With two left feet, I trip and slide,
Not quite a dance, more of a ride.

Dreams of grace, they come and go,
In frosty winds, I put on a show.
An eagle soaring? Oh wait, a goose!
With every laugh, I feel the juice.

Awkward Ballet on Frosted Grounds

A stumble here, a laugh goes there,
My inner grace just isn't fair.
With arms out wide, I start to glide,
Only to find I must collide.

The ice is calling, but I can't hear,
As friends just chuckle, their joy is clear.
My steps like jelly, all wobbly and light,
I'm a boisterous comet in the night.

Shattered Dreams and Glittering Ice

I dream of triple axels, scores so grand,
But all I manage is a faceplant stand.
The sparkles shine, the crowd enthralled,
But little do they know I've just stalled.

A flurry of laughter fills the air,
As I tumble on the icy lair.
Each cringe-worthy move brings peals of cheer,
This goofy dance brings friends so near.

Unraveled Dreams on a Slippery Path

Once I dreamed I could glide,
With elegance and style.
But ice beneath my feet,
Sends me tumbling with a smile.

With each step, my vision blurs,
As I wave to onlookers.
A graceful leap turns into flops,
And laughter fills the winter air.

Falling Stars on a Winter Stage

Underneath the twinkling lights,
I'm a comet in distress.
Each twirl's a messy battle,
In my sparkly, crashing dress.

I aimed to dazzle, spin like pros,
Yet trip on my own shoe.
The crowd erupts in joyful laughs,
While I just wave and woo.

Ballet of the Bumbling Heart

I pirouette and suddenly squeak,
Like a rubber duck set free.
My passion's strong, my balance weak,
Each move's a wobbly spree.

My partners gasp, then cheer me on,
A dance of lots of laughs.
While I spin off to the edge,
Adrift like wayward crafts.

When Skating Goes Sideways

One moment I'm upright and grand,
The next, I'm flat on my face.
The ice must be a crazy land,
Where ninjas hide with grace.

Each slip and slide, a wild ride,
With giggles as my guide.
At the end, I stand to cheer myself,
An ice queen, who's slightly misfied.

Ghosts of Elegance in a Slipstream

With flailing arms and shuffling feet,
The graceful glide feels like defeat.
A spin gone wrong, I hit the ground,
A ghost of elegance, not to be found.

Laughter echoes, my pride takes flight,
As I twirl and stumble into the night.
Those who glide with style and flair,
Whisper my name, but I'm unaware.

Blades of Ambition

I lace up tight, with dreams in my head,
My confidence high, till I trip instead.
A leap for glory, but it's a flop,
As I tumble and roll, not ready to stop.

My blades are sharp, my ambition bold,
Yet the ice is slick, and the story unfolds.
With every fall, a giggle escapes,
Creating a symphony of awkward shapes.

Hearts of Steel

With hearts of steel, we hit the rink,
Dreaming of swans, but what do we think?
I wobble and spin, a sight to behold,
While my partner grins, I'm losing control.

A crash, a thud, my dance is a fight,
Each misstep glows, in the harsh spotlight.
We're heroes of comedy, kings of the slide,
With every misstep, we take it in stride.

A Waltz with Gravity's Grin

A waltz with gravity, such a funny chase,
Each slip and slide becomes my embrace.
Round and round, like a dizzying spin,
With laughter echoing, let the fun begin.

We twirl like leaves in a comical dance,
Carefree and wild, not a single glance.
As I fall again, the ice starts to cheer,
With each clumsy move, we shed every fear.

The Misguided Pursuit of Glacial Grace

Aiming for elegance, I take the floor,
But my awkward pirouette leaves me wanting more.
With every rotation, I lose my finesse,
The crowd erupts in delightful distress.

The misguided pursuit, a quest gone amiss,
Life's slippery moments, we laugh and we kiss.
So let the ice be our stage tonight,
In clumsy chaos, we find pure delight.

Melodies of Trip and Stumble

A dance on ice, oh what a sight,
With wobbly moves, a laugh ignites.
The spin is grand, but the fall's a blast,
As laughter echoes, the memories last.

I glide with flair, then crash and roll,
Each slip's a story, a comical goal.
Round and round, I twirl with glee,
Who knew ice would play tricks on me?

Sliding into Laughter on a Gleaming Sheet

On shiny ice, I take my chance,
With a wobble and weave, I start to dance.
A courteous wave to that brave old man,
Who skates like a pro, while I'm barely a fan.

I try a glide, but hit a bump,
And land right there with a spectacular thump.
The giggles rise, can't help but snicker,
As friends join in, the fun gets thicker.

Slips and Slides in Frosty Grace

A twist and a turn, it's pure delight,
Except when I'm planning to take off in flight.
On frosty ground, I make my stand,
But gravity laughs, it's a wild ride planned.

With every fall, my courage grows,
Through laughter's lens, the joy just flows.
On this chilly stage, I twirl and glide,
With giggles and grace, there's nothing to hide.

Gliding with Two Left Feet

On the rink, where whispers roam,
I shuffle and slide, far from home.
With two left feet, I struggle and sway,
But every misstep turns night into day.

A timid skater, a wobbly soul,
Yet every tumble takes its toll.
With friends beside, I laugh out loud,
Together we stumble, proud and unbowed.

Wobbly Visions on a Shimmering Surface

With flailing arms and crooked knees,
I glide like a duck on an icy breeze.
The rink is my stage, where I dance amiss,
As friends share a laugh, I won't cease to hiss.

Around I twirl, but don't ask me how,
One misstep away from a face plant now.
A spin with a twist, but oh what a sight,
My graceful ballet is more like a fright.

Synchronized Chaos in Cold Air

We line up in rows, oh what a parade,
Each one of us destined to topple and fade.
A plan to look poised, we sway and we sway,
Together we crash, a hilarious display.

As I attempt to float, I end up in a heap,
While laughter erupts, I can barely keep.
Pogo-ing forward, with legs all tangled,
In this frosty ballet, we've all got tangled.

Mischief on a Chilly Canvas

The ice is a canvas for shenanigans wild,
With a wobble and giggle, I'm an unsteady child.
Every glide is a gamble, with perilous turns,
But joy's in the flops, and the laughter that burns.

I summon my courage with each frozen leap,
Yet I land on my back, making snow angels deep.
With grins like the Cheshire, we aim to enthrall,
In this circus of chaos, we're having a ball.

Icicles of Incompetence and Glee

Encased in my armor of warm, fuzzy wear,
I venture on ice, but with utmost despair.
Each graceful intent quickly tumbles down,
As I wave to the crowd while I wear a frown.

My feet overtake me, a shuffle of plight,
With arms like a windmill, I'm a comical sight.
Yet amidst the mishaps and giggles so free,
These icicles of blunders are dear memories for me.

Puddles of Regret on Shiny Ice

With every glide, I take a fall,
My ego crashes, oh not at all.
I swish and swirl, but then I trip,
A dance of chaos, oh what a slip.

The ice is slick, like soap on floors,
My body flails as laughter roars.
I spin around, then away I slide,
A jolly mess with nowhere to hide.

My friends all cheer as I tumble down,
A graceful prince turned to silly clown.
But in this chaos, smiles remain,
In puddles of joy, I'll trip again.

So here's to falls, each glorious laugh,
Entwined in giggles, we take a half.
Through slips and slides, we find our way,
In joyous blunders, we love to play.

Twists of Fate on Frozen Waters

I lace my skates with utmost care,
Entering the rink, feeling the air.
But oh, the ice is slick and wide,
   I spin out, welcoming the ride.

With every turn, I lose my grace,
Feet flying wild, oh what a chase.
A sudden wobble, then down I go,
   A winter tale, with comic flow.

The crowd erupts, they laugh and cheer,
A slip here, a stumble there, oh dear!
I raise my hands, a glittering sight,
   A jester's bow in the frosty light.

Though elegance is not in my fate,
I skate with joy—it's never too late.
In twists and turns, I find my fun,
   With every laugh, I'm never done.

Swaying Shadows and Tinted Dreams

I step on ice with a confident grin,
But gravity laughs, and let the fall begin.
A clumsy twirl, then a backward glide,
My shadow dances, with nowhere to hide.

Oh, look at me—elegance missed,
A flailing figure, an ice-bound twist.
I pirouette to an unseen tune,
A spectacle under the smile of the moon.

With every thud, my dreams collide,
As I bounce and roll with nowhere to guide.
In this ballet, I spin like a leaf,
Wrapped in laughter, but where's my belief?

Yet still I sway, like branches in breeze,
Mixing up joy with every unease.
In shadows of night, I twirl and gleam,
A vivid vision of funny dreams.

Unraveled Rhythms in a Frozen Frame

The music starts, I take a stance,
But rhythm escapes, I can't catch a chance.
With every beat, I lose my style,
Flopping about with a goofy smile.

My partner glides; he floats like a pro,
While I mimic jelly, just stealing the show.
We twist and tangle, a comedic sight,
An awkward duo, but hearts feel light.

A leap and a flop, then down with a thud,
Caught in a moment, trio of mud.
The crowd erupts, with glee in their eyes,
In this wacky dance, we win the prize.

So music may falter, and steps might stray,
Yet laughter rings true at the end of the day.
In our tangled mess, a joy sublime,
Unraveled rhythms, lost in time.

Laughter Echoes in the Chill

With wobbly knees, I hit the rink,
A pirouette gone wrong, I think.
My friend just fell, a sight to see,
We laugh so hard, we can't be free.

The skates are tight, my toes protest,
Each glide a gamble, a comical quest.
Twisted limbs like frozen pretzels,
We wobble on ice, creating vessel.

A spin attempt leads to more than one,
I yelp, I trip, oh what a fun!
With every fall, my joy will swell,
Laughter echoes in icy spell.

Bumps and bruises wear proud as crowns,
In our frosty kingdom, no frowns.
Snowflakes dance in our silly spree,
Here, joy and laughter are truly free.

Balancing Comically on Shimmering Ice

Wobbling forward, arms out wide,
Like a duck on skates, I glide.
With each small leap, I lose my grace,
A tumble comes, yet still I brace.

I swear I planned that awkward flip,
But down I go, and that's the trip.
Giggles bubble, the crowd's delight,
As I roll over, what a sight!

With each backspin, the cheers will rise,
Yet every twist is full of surprise.
A flailing dancer on frosty sea,
Balancing comically—just let it be!

A slip, a slide, then up I jump,
In this icy circus, I'm just a clump.
Who knew that falling could feel so grand?
With laughter flowing, I'll take my stand.

Frost-Kissed Failures and Laugh Lines

Each glide brings laughter, oh what a thrill,
As I teeter and totter, an ice-bound drill.
The rink is my canvas, I paint it with falls,
Frost-kissed failures, my biggest calls.

Hands in the air, I strike a pose,
But down I go; humor only grows.
Giggles erupt with each clumsy try,
The cold bites deeper, yet spirits fly.

I try for a jump, it's mostly a flop,
But laughter, oh laughter, it just won't stop.
Fumbling friends create a joyful scene,
In this frosty play, we dance like a dream.

With every blunder, a chuckle in kind,
In this slip-sliding world, joy's what we find.
So bring on the ice, and let the fun flow,
With frost-kissed failures, we steal the show.

When Hopes Slip Away

The ice looks so smooth, but wait and see,
With hopeful hearts, we flail with glee.
Each push is a promise, each glide a wish,
But soon we're slipping—oh, what a dish!

The hopeful leaps turn to frantic yells,
As chaos reigns with our icy spells.
We summon the courage, try one more time,
Then spiral down in a slapstick rhyme.

Comedic slips, we tumble in style,
A symphony of laughter, ice-bound guile.
Falling forward, we embrace the fate,
When hopes slip away, humor's our trait.

In this jolly mess, we find our groove,
As bodies flop and silliness moves.
With every crash, our spirits stay high,
Together we'll laugh, beneath the clear sky.

Gliding with Graceful Mishaps

Wobbly feet on slippery sheet,
A leap that lands on seat!
Hands flail like a windmill's spin,
Giggles rise from the chaos within.

Rink-bound laughter fills the air,
Lopsided spins show we don't care!
A tumble here, a crash over there,
Joyful shouts, it's all just flair.

Chasing friends and dodging the ice,
Who knew falling could be so nice?
Rookie moves, we boast with pride,
As we glide, slip, and glide.

Endless falls, yet spirits high,
With each misstep, we reach for the sky!
Tomorrow we'll conquer, or so we claim,
This frosty dance is our claim to fame.

Twirls of Clumsy Elegance

Upon the ice, we seek a waltz,
But our feet betray with careless faults.
Twists and turns, a sight bizarre,
Looks like we're training for a fall, not a star!

Attempting spins, we lose our flair,
Cartwheels happen; we barely care.
With squeaks and squeals, we bring the fun,
Our frosty ballet has just begun!

Laughter echoes, a happy crowd,
As we pirouette, we feel so proud.
With every slip, we cheer and grin,
Clumsy elegance is where we win!

Longing for grace, but finding our groove,
Turning mishaps into a new move.
As the ice creaks, we'll take our stance,
With our goofy rhythm, we take a chance.

Frosty Ballet on Shattered Dreams

We dreamed of swans but look like geese,
A frosty ballet that brings us peace.
Feet sliding out, hearts full of cheer,
Our flawed routine is the highlight here!

Whirling around, we trip with glee,
A chain reaction, oh, what a spree!
The ice won't hold our graceful quest,
Yet in this madness, we feel the best.

We sweep and swerve, but we do it loud,
Making memories that make us proud.
With every fall, our laughter transcends,
Life on the ice, where fun never ends!

So let's embrace this icy parade,
In the dance of clumsiness, we're not afraid.
With each tumble, our spirits gleam,
Who knew this mess would be a dream?

Chaotic Whirls on Frozen Ground

Beneath the lights, we make our play,
On frozen ground, we find our way.
With arms outstretched, we lose our grace,
Each wild whirl is a hilarious space!

We glide in circles, but not for long,
Our paths collide, an off-key song.
We laugh and cheer, unbothered by pride,
In this chaotic whirl, we all collide.

As we spin, we lose our hold,
Stories of our slips are retold.
A pirouette turns into a flop,
But who could resist this wild backdrop?

With every flounder, our spirits soar,
Falling flat is never a bore!
On this slippery ground, with joy profound,
Let's keep dancing, lost and found!

Grace Meets Goofiness on Ice

Wobbling around like a new-born deer,
With flailing arms, I've nothing to fear.
The crowd erupts with joyous laughter,
As I twirl and spin, then chase after disaster.

A leap that's destined to go awry,
I catch a glimpse of my friend nearby.
A slip, a slide, oh what a sight,
We're masters of chaos, pure delight!

Falling like a bag of potatoes tossed,
But every tumble just adds to the cost.
With each clap and cheer, my heart takes flight,
Who knew goofiness could feel so right?

A dance of slips beneath the moon's glow,
Sealing our fate in a comic show.
With every misstep, my spirit will soar,
In this winter wonderland, I'm begging for more.

Dancing with a Dash of Disaster

Spinning wildly, I lose my grace,
A flurry of limbs, what a funny case!
Each pirouette lands me on my back,
In this icy ballet, I've lost the track.

My friends cheer as I glide and glide,
Turning my beauty into a wild ride.
With each ill-fated twirl that I make,
I'm a jester on ice, for laughter's sake!

Fumbled and jumbled, I'm proud to be free,
Slipping like a fish that has jumped from the sea.
Chasing snowflakes while losing my shoes,
In this clumsy dance, I've nothing to lose.

Through wobbly dances and countless falls,
I conquer the ice, hear the laughter calls.
Each bounce and tumble, a thrill I'm seeking,
For every misstep, my joy is peaking!

Unsteady Feet and Joyful Falls

With unsteady feet, I bravely stride,
On this frozen canvas, what a ride!
Like a baby giraffe, a sight to behold,
Every misstep a story, every tumble bold.

I glide and swerve, feeling so grand,
Yet gravity's pull has a crazy hand.
Spinning out, with a gasp and a shout,
My graceful vision has just turned out.

Each fall is laughter, each slip a cheer,
My fellow skaters, oh so near.
Hands flying high as I tumble to ground,
In this joyful dance, my heart can be found.

So here's to the chaos of icy delight,
To unsteady feet and the laughter we invite.
In this merry mess beneath the bright lights,
We dance through the night, taking winged flights.

Frostbitten Fumbles and Fancies

Upon this ice, we dream and sway,
With frosty fumbles lighting the way.
I attempt a jump, but down I go,
The crowd erupts, what a glorious show!

Every slide's a comedy, every twist a joke,
In my slippery kingdom, I'm totally bespoke.
I'll take a bow after every pratfall,
Who knew that laughter is the best of all?

Carving through winter on a whimsy spree,
In this chilly circus, I'm the star, can't you see?
With frozen fingers but spirits so bold,
We share our stories, treasures untold.

So here's to mischief and laughter afloat,
With frostbitten fumbles, we'll never gloat.
For every crash, a memory's spun,
In this rollicking chaos, we've already won!

The Ballet of the Unsynchronized

Twirl, trip, then crash, it's quite the sight,
Gliding gracefully, but not quite right.
A toe pick here, a flail of the arms,
Landing far from charm, oh what a harm!

In perfect sync, they were not designed,
One leaps left, while another's maligned.
A pirouette gone wrong in mid-air,
A tumble, a laugh, a comical scare!

The music plays on, they strive for grace,
But find themselves in a wild chase.
Laughter erupts, as they hit the ice,
What was elegance, now isn't so nice!

With every slip, their spirits still gleam,
For awkwardness is part of their dream.
A show of bizarre, a joyful romp,
Unintended fun, a rib-tickling stomp!

Brief Encounters on a Slippery Stage

Two skaters meet, a glance, a smile,
But then one wobbles, slips a mile.
They reach for hands, it's quite the dance,
And down they go, without a chance!

They glide like ducks on a frozen pond,
With all the poise of a wayward blonde.
A sudden spin sends them both away,
And laughing echoes fill the fray!

The audience cringes, then bursts with cheer,
As every mistake becomes a souvenir.
Bound by laughter on this chilly floor,
In every fumble, they want more!

And though they tumble, roll, and feign,
Their joy in chaos is their main gain.
For every slip leads to a new height,
In this ice-bound tale of shared delight!

Where Dreams Collide with Realities

Once upon a dream, they aimed for grace,
But reality laughed, right in their face.
A leap to the stars, only to land,
With a thud on the ice, a sight so bland!

They picture the crowd, a roaring delight,
Yet end up grasping for their very right.
The vision of swans became flightless geese,
A comedy born from hopes that cease!

The judges stare, confusion unfolds,
As they land with a smack, so naturally bold.
A twirl and a fall, more rhythm than dance,
In this frosty realm, they've taken their chance!

Yet dreams still dance in their silly minds,
Each laugh and lift, in joy, it binds.
For each clumsy move is a story told,
In this fusion of dreams and the weekend cold!

Frosty Fumbles and Stumbles

A frosty morning, the sun barely shines,
Skaters step out, donning mismatched signs.
One's in a tutu, the other in gear,
As they venture forth, the end is near!

A graceful start, then a cranky glide,
With every wobble, they tangle and slide.
They attempt to impress, but what comes next?
A crash and a thud, oh, they're so vexed!

On this glacial stage, someone will fall,
With giggles erupting, echoing the hall.
A slide on one knee, a twist in mid-air,
Every stumble a tale, unfit for flair!

Yet in this chaos, their laughter will soar,
For awkwardness brings joy, that's for sure!
With frost on their cheeks, they'll call it a win,
In every fumble, a new tale begins!

Spectacle of the Clumsy Few

Whirling spins and flailing arms,
A crowd erupts in joyful charms.
With each stumble, laughter grows,
A ballet of blunders, everyone knows.

Falling down with graceful flair,
Ice chips flying everywhere.
Like tangled cats on a frozen lake,
A slapstick show, for humor's sake.

Boots that squeak and blades that slide,
A penguin's waddle is our guide.
With giggles loud, we take our turn,
To master moves we'll never learn.

At the end, we rise and cheer,
For every laugh, we hold so dear.
Through the slips and awkward spins,
The joy of falling always wins!

The Missteps of a Winter Performer

A pirouette that turned to shouts,
As graceful poise quickly routes.
With flailing limbs, I twist and shout,
This performance? Without a doubt!

Spin, slide, then bump a friend,
In this chill, there's no pretend.
With arms akimbo, I might just fly,
Or crash like winter's sad goodbye.

Frozen faces, eyes go wide,
As down I go, my pride denied.
Yet laughter rings, a joyous sound,
In this merry, frosty playground.

Socks and boots, they feel so nice,
Until I trip on my own ice.
With every flop, we find our glee,
A winter tale of hilarity!

Chaotic Harmony on Glacial Floors

Not quite ballet, but full of flair,
Each shaky glide fills the air.
Laughing at my clumsy stance,
In this madness, I still dance.

Wobbling straight into a spin,
It's hard to tell where fun begins.
My feet betray me, take a bow,
While giggles echo, here and now.

Like drunken starlings on the ice,
We twirl and slide, oh-so-nice.
With wobbly grace, we entertain,
Our winter circus dressed in gain.

When winter melts and days grow bright,
We'll cherish this hilarious plight.
In every fall, our souls take flight,
A frosty canvas, pure delight!

Cartwheeling into the Abyss

With arms like windmills, here I go,
Into the ice, a daring show.
A cartwheel planned, but fate does tease,
As I land flat with laughable ease.

Spinning wildly, losing ground,
A graceful flop is what I found.
As twinkles dance above my head,
My dreams of grace are surely dead.

Each tumble tells a comic tale,
While icy breezes start to wail.
With frozen feet that refuse to glide,
I manage still to take it in stride.

In every crash, there's joy to reap,
As laughter bubbles like fresh-baked sheep.
While gliding dreams meet their demise,
I'll laugh beneath these endless skies!

Skating into a Laughable Abyss

Gliding with grace, or so I thought,
My feet had other plans, I was caught.
With a wobble and twist, I took to flight,
A frosty ballet, a comical sight.

Friends doubled over, they couldn't contain,
As I pirouetted, but fell with a gain.
A spin that transformed into a fumble,
Who knew such missteps could cause such a tumble?

Laughter erupted, I embraced the fall,
Each slip on the ice was a carnival ball.
Shimmies and shakes, my skills came undone,
A skate in each hand, I was far from done!

The rink became home to my fanciful flops,
As I danced with the zamboni, continuous hops.
In this waltz of disaster, who needs to be great?
As long as I smile, I can't tempt fate.

The Gravity of Laughs on Ice

With a flourish I stepped on the icy expanse,
My friends cheered aloud, 'Give it a chance!'
But gravity laughed, it had other plans,
And down I went with no skill or stance.

Twirls turned to tumbles, like leaves in a race,
My body a canvas, a slapstick embrace.
The upside-down skating was quite a display,
Even clumsy old penguins should learn from my way.

One foot in front, the other now trailing,
I attempted a jump, oh, it was a failing.
The ice had a grip, oh, such fierce embrace,
My flailing limbs painted the air like a vase.

But laughter's my partner, we glide hand in hand,
In this slippery dance, I take my own stand.
Though I may be awkward, my heart's full of cheer,
With each laugh I conquer, my panic disappears.

Misadventures in Glitter and Frost

Dressed like a star for my ice-bound debut,
With sparkles and sequins, I'd steal the view.
But with each little twirl, I felt the demise,
My outfit a hazard, oh, what a surprise!

Attempting a lunge, I'd look suave while bold,
But I danced like a marionette gone uncontrolled.
Each glitter-filled fall was a sight to behold,
More laughter erupted than had ever been told.

The skaters around me, with skills finely honed,
Marveled at elegance while I just bemoaned.
A twinkle, a tangle, I glid and I slipped,
In a blizzard of glitter, my ego was clipped.

Yet still I persisted, I jumped and I pranced,
Each ludicrous moment was part of the dance.
With each crash and tumble into the frosty abyss,
I learned it was laughs that I didn't want to miss.

Cautionary Tales from the Rink

A bright flashing sign warned me, 'Proceed with care,'
But I strapped on my skates with an overconfident flair.
With a leap and a sail, I dashed with delight,
Only to land flat, what a comical plight!

The bucket of ice on my head was a twist,
As spectators laughed, through the chaos I whist.
Each wobble and lurch was a tale to unfold,
Of caution gone awry, a boldness too bold.

I tangled my legs, my ankles did scream,
What I thought was a glide turned into a meme.
With each flailing try, the spectators roared,
A caution to heed, or laughter stored!

But here's the grand secret, as silly as it seems,
In the folly of skating, I caught all the dreams.
For laughter is magic, on ice it will bloom,
In a world filled with laughter, there's always more room.

When Grace Meets Gravity

On blades so fine, I take my stand,
With wobbly knees, I hope for grand.
A dainty glide turns into a flop,
As gravity grins and makes me stop.

With little control, I circle wide,
A pirouette quickly turns to a slide.
The crowd erupts, I hear their cheer,
Amidst my flailing, I cringe in fear.

A twinkle-toed fairy I long to be,
But I'm more like a bumblebee.
With every slip I take a leap,
And promise myself, "No more steep!"

Yet laughter dances upon my face,
As I fumble through this icy space.
Each tumble earned a laugh or two,
In my clumsy world, I'll still skate through.

Whirls and Twirls of a Shaky Heart

With socks too tight and laces loose,
I venture forth, I've made my noose.
My heart is pounding, my breath is quick,
As on the ice, I attempt a trick.

A faux pas here, a crash down there,
My dreams of grace, a breath of air.
Spinning wildly, I lose my way,
In a whirlwind of chaos, I sway.

The crowd erupts in raucous glee,
At my expense, oh woe is me!
A shaky heart, with boundless cheer,
As I rock the rink without much fear.

But oh, what fun in each rude fall,
With laughter echoing, I stand tall.
Next time I'll nail a triple axel,
Or maybe just stick to the castle.

Jesters of the Ice

The ice is cold, my feet are sore,
As I glide and trip, I beg for more.
I'm a jester here, with a floppy grin,
In this wild circus, I jump right in.

A spin and a hop, I leap and sway,
Landing on my rear, what a display!
The audience chuckles, oh what a sight,
As I stumble over, trying to be light.

With every slip, I steal the show,
Waving my arms like a penguin in tow.
A merry dance of blunders and falls,
In this winter wonderland, laughter calls.

I cherish each chuckle, each grimace and grin,
For in my frosty folly, I am a win.
A true entertainer, though not by design,
With each joyful fall, I claim this line.

Misguided Spins in the Cold

A flip of the skirt, a raise of the blade,
I grip the railing, feeling dismayed.
With each frosty turn, my confidence wanes,
In a lopsided ballet, my dignity pains.

A two-step forward, then back I go,
Like a clumsy calf on a winter show.
With serious intent, I try for a glide,
Yet ice-borne mischief decides to collide.

My friends cheer loudly, oh what a thrill,
But I'm twirling in circles, losing my will.
The cold air bites, my cheeks burn bright,
While my flailing limbs create quite a sight.

Despite my wild dance on this frozen expanse,
I laugh at the chaos, unwilling to chance.
For when things go awry, what's left to withhold?
In misguided spins, what fun to behold!

A Tumult of Twirls and Miscalculations

Spinning like a dizzy top,
Skates slip, and I might flop.
A flurry of flails, oh what a sight,
Wobbling around, I've lost my fight.

With arms flailing like a bird,
Each graceful curve a bit absurd.
I'm mastering the art of falling down,
As laughter echoes all around.

A leap that ends in icy grace,
Rolling on the ground, I find my place.
The crowd erupts, a joyful cheer,
For every tumble, they draw near.

In a frozen ballet gone awry,
I twirl and spin with a comical cry.
Yet amid the chaos, joy does bloom,
As I glide and slide, a clown in the room.

Laughter Carried by the Winter Wind

Gliding forth with hopeful glee,
A solid crack under me,
With every twist, a smile wide,
I wobble, but I still glide.

Snowflakes dance like twinkling lights,
As I attempt some daring flights.
A leap that led to quite a fall,
Laughter echoing, I hear it all.

Friends chuckle as I try again,
Spinning wildly, dodging pain.
Grace is a dream, yet here I stand,
Embracing the stumbles, oh so grand.

Winter whispers secrets sweet,
As joy and laughter find their beat.
On frozen lakes, we all unite,
In a comedy of slips tonight.

The Dance of Faux Poise

With confidence high, I take a stride,
But soon find balance has left my side.
Swaying like a graceful tree,
My faux poise is a sight to see.

Pirouettes turn to spins and slips,
My control fades with frantic quips.
Each moment's laughter fuels the show,
A comedic turn in the frosty glow.

Arms akimbo, I chase my dreams,
Only to crash, bursting at the seams.
It's not perfection but joy I seek,
With every tumble, I laugh and squeak.

So let them watch my wild routine,
A frosty ballet that's far from serene.
In faux poise, I find delight,
As laughter carries through the night.

The Icy Symphony of Mismatched Steps

A symphony of thuds and squeaks,
As I attempt those fancy peaks.
Two left feet on this frozen stage,
A comic dancer at any age.

Colliding skates, a jarring beat,
Imitating swans with little feat.
Laughter erupts as I lose control,
In this disconnected icy stroll.

Choreography lost in the fray,
Twisting and turning, but not my way.
Each twist a giggle, each slip a cheer,
As winter's whimsy draws friends near.

So here I dance with all my heart,
This dazzling chaos, a true work of art.
In mismatched steps, we find our flow,
Creating memories with a frosty glow.

Cracks beneath the Feet of Aspirants

With every wobbly step they take,
A hopeful grip, a silent quake.
The ice, it laughs with each slip and slide,
As dreams of grace begin to hide.

Flailing arms that reach for air,
Like swans transformed to clumsy bears.
Each spin intended, a new dance sought,
Yet tumble and slide, is the lesson taught.

The newcomers glide on their own feet,
A little laugh, a little defeat.
With every crash, they learn the game,
In this chill, no one's afraid of shame.

So here's to those who dare to try,
When balance wins, and patterns lie.
The laughter echoes, the ice holds tight,
For all who stumble, oh what a sight!

Elegant Chaos in Frosty Air

Spinning wildly with glee they mess,
Ballet dreams turned to pure distress.
With flailing limbs like windmills' grace,
Each pirouette a wild embrace.

The frosty breath makes giggles bloom,
Bringing joy amidst the room.
They glide like penguins, proud yet shy,
Chasing laughter beneath the sky.

A ballet of shoes, two left and right,
Creating art with every slight.
Each twist and turn is sure to show,
That elegance is far from pro.

So let them spin and shake the noise,
In icy chaos, everyone enjoys.
The frosty air holds laughter near,
For all who dare, there's nothing to fear!

The Fable of the Fumbled Skate

Once upon a time on ice so slick,
A crew of skaters learned each trick.
With blades that danced in the chilly light,
But soon they turned this grace to fright.

They aimed for spins but landed plops,
As laughter rang from shocked ice tops.
Each chosen move a fumbled score,
On the rink, they tumbled more and more.

Legs intertwine, a jumbled lot,
Chasing glory, accumulating knots.
What once was art became a fun spree,
A fable told with much glee.

So gather 'round and share the tale,
Of mishaps wild in frosty gale.
For all who skate with hearts so bold,
In frosty chaos, memories unfold!

An Overture of Unruly Glides

Across the rink, the giggles soar,
As dancers slip and search for more.
An overture of jumbled fun,
Each glide a quest that's never done.

With arms flailing like overcooked pasta,
They spin and dodge in a chilly rasta.
A strategy born from purest jest,
As they navigate this dizzying quest.

Wobbling to music, feet out of sync,
Eyes meet and giggles primed to blink.
In every duck-walk and comic blunder,
Lies the warmth of laughter, a joyful thunder.

So raise a cheer for those who try,
To glide on ice and dare to fly.
In every tumble, and laughter wide,
Is the charm of skating, our joy and pride!

Fractured Pirouettes Under Stars

Under the moon, I tried to twirl,
My skates betrayed, I took a whirl.
With arms flailing, I lost my grip,
I spun like a fish on an icy trip.

Laughter erupted from all around,
As I crashed down without a sound.
Feet tangled up in an awkward mess,
Trying to dance in this frosty dress.

Snowflakes giggled as I tumbled wide,
Each glide a battle, a slippery ride.
A pirouette turned into a plop,
Watch my comedy show, I won't stop!

Under the stars, I'll proudly fall,
Embracing the chaos through it all.
With every slip, my joy ignites,
This frosty stage is pure delight!

A Slippery Serenade of Swaying Feet

Beneath the lights, I took a chance,
In shiny skates, I dared to dance.
With every wobbly glide, I sway,
A serenade of slipping hay.

My feet a jigsaw, mismatched and sore,
Spinning round, oh, look! There's more!
A twist, a turn, then whoops, look out!
I'm down again, surrounded by doubt.

Frosty air filled with giggles and cheer,
My flailing arms gave everyone fear.
But laughter's the song that fills this place,
As I tumble again with an awkward grace.

Each pass a treasure, each fall a thrill,
Slipping and sliding is such a skill.
With every mishap, I only find bliss,
In this frosty ballet, it's hard to miss!

Jesters on a Frosted Stage

Here on the ice, we give it a try,
With dazzling mishaps that make us fly.
A jester's heart in this glacial plight,
We wobble and twirl, oh, what a sight!

Laughter echoes like a winter song,
With every slip, we can't go wrong.
Cracks in the ice are my best friends,
Together we laugh, our joy never ends.

With floppy hats and frozen toes,
Each graceful flop in rhythm flows.
Around we go, a parade of grace,
In our charming chaos, we find our place.

Jesters we are, on this slick stage,
In clumsy ballet, we'll always engage.
So bring on the slip-ups, let's dance away,
For laughter is the magic we display!

Comedic Glides Over Frozen Paths

On frozen paths, we take our glide,
With stiffened limbs and hearts filled with pride.
Yet every turn shouts a playful joke,
As we wobble and bounce like some wild bloke.

Hands flailing wildly, our balance is woeful,
Each leap we make is equally colorful.
While striding with flair, oh what a vision,
A farcical dance is our true mission.

Round and round like pinwheeled toys,
With each little tumble, we find the poise.
Crashing softly, we laugh out loud,
Comedic glides, we're so very proud.

With every laugh, the cold disappears,
In joyful chaos, we forget our fears.
So leap and slide, let's make some cheer,
For comedy reigns when we're all near.

Laughter and Tears on Shattered Ice

With wobbly feet, I glide and sway,
Flailing limbs in a frosty ballet.
A tumble here, a stumble there,
My skates declare I'm in disrepair.

Friends laugh loud, as I spin and fall,
A sight so grand, they're having a ball.
Each icy plunge fuels giggles and cheer,
My graceful dreams disappeared this year.

Winter's chill wraps me in a thrall,
Yet laughter brightens this frosty brawl.
Through shouts and laughs, I find my place,
In this awkward dance, I claim my space.

So here's to slips and the joy they bring,
Skating's a blast, even when I sting.
With every fall, I rise with glee,
An artist of ice, barely carefree.

The Icy Lament of a Dreamer

I dreamed of skating like a feathered swan,
But my feet have minds of their own, oh, the con!
The ice is my canvas, but I paint in slips,
A masterpiece built with fumbled trips.

I close my eyes to feel the wind's caress,
But open them wide, oh what a mess!
With lines of chaos, I carve my own fate,
An artist of awkward, can't seem to relate.

Spinning dreams twirl, then crash to the floor,
A symphony played by a clumsy spore.
With laughter as music, I dance in despair,
Here in this rink, I find humor to share.

Each flailing moment, a joy to recall,
A dreamer on ice, I may not enthrall.
But as I tumble and sway with delight,
I cherish the fun of my frosty fight.

Mismatched Steps on Slippery Grounds

On slippery grounds, I take my stance,
With mismatched steps in my chilly dance.
A pirouette gone dramatically wrong,
My skate got tangled as I tried to prolong.

Laughter erupts from a nearby tree,
The birds are mocking, it's plain to see.
I wave at the crowd, gracefully lame,
In this slippery saga, I hope for some fame.

With cold air nipping at my hopeful nose,
I muster the courage as my patience grows.
A shuffle, a slide, an awkward turn,
Each falling trip is a lesson to learn.

Yet joy is found in each failing feat,
In this frosty arena where laughter is sweet.
So I'll keep on skating without any shame,
For life's a rough rink, but I love the game.

Balancing Act in the Frosted Arena

In the frosted arena, I take a deep breath,
Balance feels fragile, like a dancer with death.
I sway left and right, a new kind of prance,
Then whirl in a moment, and fall in a trance.

The crowd is now roaring, tears in their eyes,
At not-so-fine art resembling clumsy cries.
I stand back up, with spirit to spare,
To conquer the ice with a bold, foolish flair.

As I glide on the edges of fate's frozen blade,
Each slip an adventure, a comical parade.
So here's to the echoes of laughter and fun,
In the frosted arena, my joy's never done.

With frosty friendships and giggles galore,
I'll embrace every stumble, I'm ready for more.
For in every misstep lies stories to tell,
In this balancing act, I'm doing quite well.

Ballet of the Blundering Skater

On frozen fields, I take my stance,
With wobbly legs, I start to prance.
A twirl, a spin, then off I go,
Straight into snow, like a one-horse show.

The crowd erupts in laughter loud,
As I gracefully thud, I'm feeling proud.
A pirouette, oh what a sight,
More like a tumble, than pure delight.

A graceful leap? My dreams take flight!
Yet gravity wins; what a sorry sight!
I clasp my skates, ready to sway,
But trip on my lace and cartwheel away.

With arms in the air, I bow to all,
A final grand gesture before I fall.
All I wanted was a flair to show,
Instead, I'm the star of a slapstick show.

Slipstream Serenade of the Awkward

Gliding smoothly, or so I thought,
My legs do a dance, but coordination's naught.
A slip and a slide, I lose my groove,
The ice is my stage, but I can't improve.

With each hopeful stride, the ice does mock,
As I flail and thrash, like a fish out of dock.
A slide for my grace, a stumble for flair,
Each spin is an accident, I swear, I swear!

One grand jeté, I really believe,
But I prop myself up, my pride takes leave.
The edges bite, my skates do protest,
As I roll and I tumble, I'm simply a mess.

But laughter erupts, from all far and wide,
As I'm dubbed the champion of the slide.
With echoes of giggles, I finally know,
It's not how you skate, but the fun in the show.

Frosted Folly on a Grand Stage

The spotlight shines, my turn to shine,
With a wink and a smile, I take to the line.
No graceful glide, just a stumble and twist,
I'm a frosted jester; oh, how can I resist?

As I leap for glory, I adopt a fine pose,
But the ice has its plans, and down I goes!
A flurry of arms, I create a swirl,
Call me a snowstorm, I'm in a whirl!

A bump and a crash, a dramatic flair,
The audience gasps, then erupts in air.
What happens next is truly a treat,
I belly-slide through, all joy and defeat.

Yet somehow I'm laughing, no need to complain,
As I gather myself, feeling slightly insane.
Each fall is a chapter, a tale of the night,
In this frosted folly, I shine just right.

The Confessions of a Seasonal Skater

With skates on my feet, I bravely depart,
Hoping to shine, oh, where do I start?
Each winter I promise sleigh bells will ring,
Instead I just find myself, fumbling with bling.

My friends take the ice, with elegance grand,
While I'm in the corner, trying to stand.
A salute for the pro, then off I glide,
But not for long, as I slip and slide!

A hesitant glide, a leap gone awry,
I've got all the grace of a pig in the sky.
I'm here for the fun, the laughter and cheer,
But my flailing limbs create a circus here!

So here are my secrets, my follies laid bare,
Embrace every tumble, it's all just a dare.
For laughter and joy are the true winning score,
In the world of the ice, I'll always want more!

Whimsical Wobbles Under Frosted Skies

With blades that glide on ice so slick,
I twist and twirl, oh what a trick.
A spin, a slip, I'm lost in glee,
As ice beneath my feet shouts, "Flee!"

A penguin dance on frozen stream,
I wobble round, a frosty dream.
I wave to crowds, they watch and laugh,
My frosty ballet, the world's true gaffe.

A chin up high, I strike a pose,
But oh, here comes my trusty toes!
With grace I tumble, like a sack of flour,
Unplanned acrobatics, my finest hour.

Yet through the falls and icy yells,
A joy fills hearts, a giggling spell.
For in this slip, I find a cheer,
Embracing all that bring us here.

A Haphazard Waltz in Winter's Grip

I twirled around with outstretched arms,
But something gave, oh winter's charms!
I soared like kites, not quite in flight,
Now I'm a snowman, what a sight!

The music played, the skaters glide,
While I just cling to a snowy ride.
Each move a venture, every slip divine,
A dance of chaos, how I shine!

With laughter loud, my friends can share,
As I attempt a pirouette in air!
The ground comes quickly, it knows my name,
In this grand waltz, perhaps I'm lame.

Yet joy breaks free from every fall,
As giggles rise, I hear their call.
In this wild slip upon the rime,
I'll laugh and skate, it's silly time!

Laughing with the Fates of Frost

Oh what a sight, I grin and spin,
The ice is calling, let the fun begin!
I grab my mate, let's set a scene,
We wobble forth, the clumsy queens!

The frosty wind shrieks, it's out to play,
As I take a leap; will I fly away?
My flailing arms, a sight to behold,
Truth be told, I'm more than bold.

With every twist, the laughter grows,
A frosty giggle, my mishaps show.
In this wild spin, I find my grace,
With every fall, I've found my place.

The ice, it chuckles, the stars align,
In haphazard moments, we all can shine.
Our wobbles tell a tale so grand,
As laughter echoes in this frosty land.

Falling with Style in a Frozen Dream

A leap, a bound, oh what a thrill,
I soar like snowflakes, then tumble down hill.
In winter's embrace, I'm full of cheer,
With every spin, I shed a tear.

Oh, the elegance of my great fail,
Like a prancing deer, or a slippery snail.
I break into laughter, my face aglow,
As I glide through puddles of icy woe.

My friends are near, they call my name,
As chaos rules, it's all a game.
One wrong turn, and suddenly I'm free,
In this frozen ballet, blissful, yet silly.

So join me now, embrace the glide,
With wild abandon, we take this ride.
For falling with style is what we choose,
On this frosty stage, we'll never lose.

Frosty Follies: A Comedic Ice Saga

Wobbly ankles on a frozen lake,
Flailing arms give all a heartache.
Falling hard, a flurry of snow,
Laughter erupts in every toe.

Spinning in circles like a wild whirligig,
Making snow angels, oh so big.
With every slip and every slide,
A merry dance we cannot hide.

Chasing friends, yet losing the race,
Face-planting into cold, wet space.
Giggles echo as we collide,
Laughter is our winter guide.

The ice becomes a laughter stage,
Where all our blunders turn a page.
A comedy show on frozen cheer,
Together we melt away the fear.

When the Glider Becomes the Glum

Stepping out with utmost pride,
One bold move, then off I glide.
But wait! What's that? A slip, a yelp!
I'm now the punchline, oh, help!

My graceful spin turns into flops,
With every twirl, my confidence drops.
A sassy dip becomes a face plant,
A disaster dance, my pride now cant.

Watch me wobble, watch me sway,
I promise it's my unique display.
As I crash into snow-covered trees,
Laughter erupts, I'm the clown, oh please!

Yet in this blunder, joy ignites,
Where laughter blooms and hope invites.
So bring your chuckles, let's not be glum,
For it's all in the fun, however we come!

The Icy Tale of Uncoordinated Dreams

In a world where grace is king,
I'm the jester trying to sing.
Skates on feet, but still I trip,
A silly dance, a wobbly flip.

Around I go, like a wild kite,
My balance wavers, oh what a sight!
I attempt a jump, and oh dear me,
I land with flair, like a falling tree!

Cheering crowds, or so I thought,
It's just my friends, all laughing a lot.
With every tumble, the smiles grow wide,
In this icy realm, we all slide.

A skater's dream? Perhaps not quite,
But in every fall, we find delight.
With a chuckle and cheer, we glide once more,
In this frosty tale, laughter's the core!

A Clumsy Heart in a Crystal Realm

With a heart full of hopes, I step on the ice,
Each glide feels like rolling dice.
I leap and spin, my fate in doubt,
A grand performance? Not what it's about!

My feet betray me, oh what a mess,
Unruly motions, I must confess.
A cartwheel gone wrong, I twist and shout,
As friends fall down, we've got clouts!

The smell of the popcorn drifts in the air,
As I stumble and slip without a care.
Mirthful moments fill the chilly haze,
In this comic dance, we find our praise.

At the end of the day, as we join hands,
Collect our giggles, make foolish plans.
With every blunder, we joyfully heal,
In this frosty realm, it's laughter we feel!